TIARAS past and present

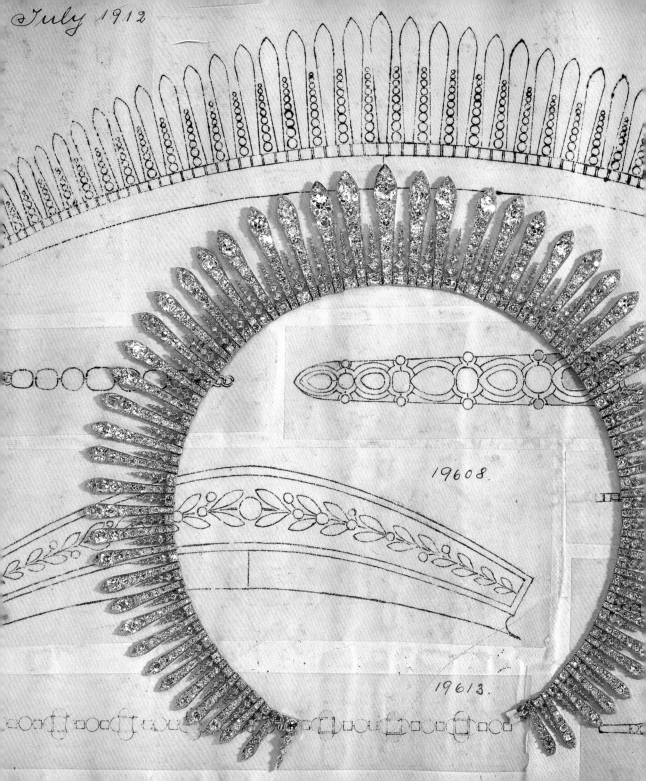

July 1912

19608.

19613.

9604

1960

19

1961

First published by V&A Publishing, 2002

Paperback edition published 2008

V&A Publishing
Victoria and Albert Museum
South Kensington
London SW7 2RL

Distributed in North America by Harry N. Abrams,
Inc., New York

© The Board of Trustees of the Victoria and Albert
Museum, 2002

The moral right of the author has been asserted.

Library of Congress Control Number 2007935519

ISBN 978 1 85177 534 7

10 9 8 7 6 5 4
2014 2013 2012

A catalogue record for this book is available from
the British Library.

Designed by Broadbase
Special photography by Keith Davey of Prudence
Cuming Associates

Printed in China

V&A Publishing
Supporting the world's leading
museum of art and design,
the Victoria and Albert
Museum, London

Front cover Photograph by Elena
Segatini, Woman putting on tiara.
© Elena Segatini Bloom/CORBIS.

Back cover Five stars tiara
supported on a gallery of stylized
foliage (see pl.24, p.35).
Private Collection

Page 1 Art Nouveau taste platinum
tiara. Probably by Cartier, c.1900.
Fred Leighton, New York.

Page 2 Diamond fringe tiara/
necklace mounted in gold and set
in silver. Sheet of designs dated
July 1912 by E. Wolff & Co.,
manufacturing jewellers, London.
Private Collection, and E. Wolfe & Co.

contents

THE tiara might easily be regarded today as something of a fashion dinosaur. Scintillating shamelessly with hugely valuable precious stones, it is cumbersome and outmoded. Completely beyond the hopes and dreams of most women, it is an emblem of inherited rank, deservedly redundant in an increasingly democratic world.

In reality nothing could be further from the truth. This elegant and fascinating form of jewellery is not a fossil but rather a sleeping beauty betrayed by far more than just a flickering pulse. And at the present time, the dawn of a new millennium, interest in the tiara is enormous, promising a fresh era of startling versatility.

The origins of this, the noblest and most flattering of all jewels, are almost as remote as those of civilization itself. Indeed, it may be that we have always felt the desire to adorn the head, the centre of intelligence and the source of emotional expression. Before the evolution of metallurgy, primitive peoples made garlands and wreaths from flowers and foliage – just as today children, friends and lovers may encircle each other's heads with humble daisy chains on a summer's afternoon. Over time, these flowers and plants were accorded their own emblematic meanings – the victorious were crowned with laurel, and newly-weds with myrtle – while the wreaths and garlands acquired their own social and ritual associations.

Just as humankind has found the very transience of nature's beauty so haunting, the timelessness and permanence of precious metals and stones have had

1 *Le Masque Japonais,* by Alfred Stevens, c.1874. Two young guests have strayed away from the assembled company, their curiosity aroused by a grotesque mask displayed on the wall. In the foreground, an unmarried woman, modestly wearing gloves, has dressed her hair simply with flowers. Behind her, a young bride, wearing a tiara, gazes knowingly at the gaping mask. The tiara, with its centuries-old cultural associations, is central to our understanding of the painting's deeper meaning, as it is only worn by married women. John Mitchell & Son Fine Paintings, London.

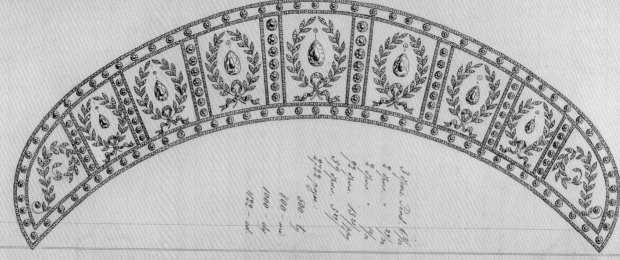

the same effect, as they seem to defy the inexorability of natural decay. As soon as craftsmen developed the necessary skill and techniques, they transmuted these temporary floral ornaments into potentially everlasting forms. Ironically, however, few tiaras from the ancient civilizations survive, and many of the most beautiful examples made in the last two centuries have been broken up when they became outmoded, so that their precious stones could be removed and reincorporated into more wearable items. Sometimes the only traces we have left are paintings, photographs and illustrations in jewellers' record books. Others have been adapted so much as they passed from generation to generation that it is difficult to attribute a provenance to them with any authority.

The origins of a number of tiaras still in existence lie with the old royal families of Europe, and as such play their own part in history; inevitably some serve as poignant reminders of lives shattered by revolution or personal misfortune. Others, sometimes of quite humble origins, speak of victory and happiness, or bear intimate messages of love; they have acquired their own mystique from their original owners and the bizarre occasions on which they were worn.

2, 3 Designs from the record books of Fabergé's chief jewellery workmaster, Holmström. *(Top)* A grand sapphire and diamond tiara in the Old Russian taste. At the centre of the composition are impressive, drop-shaped cabochon-cut stones. Dated 1912. *(Below)* An openwork diamond-set kokoshnik arranged in the Louis XVI taste as a graduated frieze of laurel wreaths emblematic of the Triumph of Love. Dated 1909. Wartski, London.

In the evolution of its design, the tiara tells its own social and cultural history. Unlike the dinosaur, it has adapted to changes – in both fashion and society – and survived. Tiaras may have been inconspicuous in recent years, but their future is in good hands. It is, after all, the designers, with their breathtakingly beautiful creations, who understand the tiara's potential, knowing that nothing else can make a woman feel or look as special as these elegant and dramatic jewels.

from ANCIENT to MODERN

ACCORDING to legend, it was the Greek god Dionysus who invented the head ornament we call the diadem. Certainly, the word itself is derived from the Greek (*'diadein'*, to bind around), although head ornaments made from bound foliage and flowers, and later metal, were characteristic of other ancient civilizations such as the Etruscans and the Scythians. The Ancient Greeks had only limited access to gold, from northern Kazakstan and the Altai Mountains, until Alexander the Great reached the main gold-supplying regions of the Persian Empire in 331 BC. Greek craftsmen were quick to exploit its malleability and transform head-dresses of living flowers into everlasting garlands fashioned from gleaming yellow metal. It must have seemed as though these finely wrought wreaths and circlets had been sent to earth by the very gods themselves.

Several types of head ornament were made in Ancient Greece, but the diadems mostly took the form of bands with pediments. Etruscan wreaths and diadems were tighter and more conventional, while the head-dress of the Scythian people, the kokoshnik, resembled a stiff halo. This last ancient prototype was to prove just as enduring as its Mediterranean counterparts, although its sphere of influence was more limited. It was assimilated into Russian folk costume, but became a popular model for Western European tiara design in the 19th and 20th centuries. The word 'tiara' is actually Persian in origin – the name first denoted the high-peaked head-dresses of Persian kings, which were encircled by 'diadems' (bands of purple and white decoration). Now it is used to describe almost every form of decorative head ornament.

Although there are accounts of special occasions on which men wore necklaces and gold wreaths, jewellery was more usually worn by women. In time,

4 *Mummy portrait of a woman*, attributed to the Isidora Master, Romano-Egyptian, c. AD 100–110; encaustic and gilt on a wooden panel wrapped in linen. The gold wreath she wears in her hair is part of an elaborate collection of jewellery; earrings set with pearls, an amethyst pendant, and two necklaces of emerald beads.
© The J. Paul Getty Museum.

5 A tiara, probably Italian, made in the Roman taste as a garland of roses cut from sheet gold, c.1815. The flowers are heightened with turquoise, pink topaz, emeralds, diamonds, amethysts and pearls. This jewel can be divided to make it shorter, and the extra gold ribbon ties required are kept within the case. Private Collection. Photograph Wartski.

6 A tiara of oxidized silver decorated with gold eglantines, the centres of which are set with rose-cut diamonds. The flower heads are mounted *en tremblant*, and may be removed and worn in the hair as single ornaments (the pins needed for this are concealed in the base of the case). The design of this tiara is inspired by the wreaths worn by the Ancient Greeks, which were made of beaten gold and date back to the 3rd century BC. Made by the French firm of Pardonneau and Daumesnil, jewellers to the Prince of Wales and the King of the Belgians, c.1880. Anne Schofield. Photograph Wartski.

gold wreaths and diadems became reserved for more ambitious and showy occasions, and the tiara's association with privilege and ostentation continues to prevail.

It is frustrating that only a few images of women wearing diadems have survived from this time. One of the most significant is a gold disc from South Russia depicting Athena, goddess of war, wearing a helmet fronted by a diadem decorated with scrollwork, which suggests that such head ornaments have always been an emblem of high rank. Wreaths were also offered as tribute to the deities and used as bullion, decorating temples and shrines and adding greatly to their wealth. Whenever possible, they were made of golden foliage that was sacred to a particular god. Ivy was for Dionysus and wheat for Demeter, but nothing less than oak would do for Zeus himself.

The Romans were great admirers of the skill and artistry of the Greeks, and emulated them in many ways, not least in their taste for wreaths and diadems. Although, in comparison, Roman craftsmanship lacked the delicacy so admired in ancient Greek and Etruscan jewellery, their jewelled head-dresses more than made up for it in theatrical effect. This may indeed have been the aim. The most important part the Romans played in the evolution of the tiara, however, was in their pioneering use of precious stones. Amethysts and pearls, emeralds, sapphires and even diamonds gradually became available to Roman craftsmen as the Empire expanded. The intense colours and refractive qualities of these stones started to play a central part in jewellery design. As in Greece, foliate and floral head-dresses remained popular throughout this time, however, and although the gods with which they were associated were Roman, the emblematic meanings given to the leaves and flowers stayed largely the same.

7 A tiara of oak leaves, acorns and hollow acorn cups designed in the manner of Ancient Greek jewellery, set with a profusion of brilliant- and rose-cut diamonds. Made by Garrard after the neo-classical fashion of the early 19th century for the 15th Duke of Norfolk to give his bride, Gwendolen Constable Maxwell, on the occasion of their marriage in 1904. Private Collection.

8 A tiara of rock crystal engraved with arabesques in the Old Russian taste, made by Cartier for Baron Pierre de Gunsburg in February 1912. The panels of lapidary-work are mounted in platinum and decorated with three ornamental motifs of rose- and brilliant-cut diamonds, and the jewel is surmounted by a line of graduated old-cut coloured diamonds and a line of brilliant-cut diamonds in *mille grain* settings. The base is defined with a line of rose-cut diamonds in a similar setting. The shape of this tiara is that of a true kokoshnik – the traditional Russian headdress that is generally made of velvet overlaid and embroidered with ornaments, often rising to a pinnacle at the front. Private Collection.

We have some record of how this jewellery was worn in the last years of the Empire from the remarkable portraits painted on the mummy cases that have survived from Egypt's first Roman period (Plate 4). These mummy cases, which rank among the greatest works of art that have passed down to us from ancient times, frequently depict the deceased wearing pearl earrings, amuletic Medusa-head necklaces and raw emerald crystal beads. Gold wreaths of laurel leaves and berries are worn by both men and women; these were often intended to symbolize the hope of triumph over death.

With the spread of Christianity and the waning of the Eastern Roman Empire, the wearing of wreaths and diadems gradually declined and eventually ceased. Although they were represented in painting and sculpture during the inter-vening years, they were not revived as part of dress until the late 18th century. The reasons why such a flattering jewel should have lapsed into relative obscurity for so long are complex. Its disappearance was partly to do with the need for an outward show of Christian piety at a time when even oblique references to the ancient world carried associations of immorality and libertinism. Women of fashion were denied the pleasure of the tiara's elegance and its flattering effects until the advent of neo-classicism and the court fashions of the First Empire restored it to respectability.

9 (*below*) A bandeau made by Cartier in the Persian taste. It dismantles to make a brooch and matching bracelets. Private Collection.

10 (*opposite*) A Spartan diadem of gilt metal set with green and white pastes. This neo-classical jewel was once owned by Dame Ellen Terry, then by Dame Joan Sutherland. Miss Joanna Lumley, O.B.E.

LOVE and MARRIAGE

THERE can be few social customs as powerfully symbolic as the crowning of a bride's head on her wedding day. Her head-dress signifies the loss of innocence and the triumph of love, and has played an integral part in nuptial ceremonies, in many traditions and many cultures, for thousands of years. Even in the most modern and sophisticated societies, this head-dress often continues to take the form of a simple garland of flowers. But it is the tiara that remains the most striking emblem of such a central rite of passage in the Western world.

11 *A Votive Offering to Cupid* (c.1767), by Jean-Baptiste Greuze. The French genre and portrait painter Jean-Baptiste Greuze, whose works were popular in the period before the French Revolution, specialized in allegories of love and in studies of girls who found themselves in troublesome situations in their pursuit of it. In this instance, a supplicant Roman girl makes a promise to a statue of Cupid, who in return crowns her with a floral garland. The daisies at the foot of the painting are emblematic of innocence, whilst the roses of Venus are cut and have already started to fade. The overturned vessel provides a perch for Venus's doves. This amusing picture shows how the garland, and by extension, the tiara – worn only by married women – are associated with the crowning of love. The Wallace Collection, London.

In England, the custom of wearing jewelled head ornaments at weddings was well established by the end of the 15th century. By this time, crowns were no longer seen as the exclusive privilege of royalty but as a symbol of the dignity and joy of wedlock, and sometimes precious metal circlets were given just to mark a betrothal. Frequently made up of trefoil-shaped fleurons, nuptial ornaments were redolent of Gothic architecture and the Christian ideals it incorporated.

For the vast majority of modern women, their wedding is probably the only occasion in their life when they can wear a tiara without fear of looking incongruous. Such an opportunity is likely to be as eagerly anticipated as any other part of the day's arrangements, as the tiara, the most elegant and dramatic of all jewels, has the unique ability to make a bride feel and look the centre of attention. It is the endorsement of her status as queen of the day. Even the humblest of wedding suppliers carries a varied range of jewelled head ornaments;

and if the bride's family is fortunate enough to have sufficient means, the tiara will be gem-set. The choice of stones is particularly important as, according to the ancient lore of the lapidary, different stones carry special meanings. Flowers, too, convey a variety of symbolic messages. Just as in antiquity various plants and flowers were considered to be attributes of individual gods and goddesses, so in the modern world a similar system was devised that came to be known as 'the language of flowers'. Each and every bloom carried a covert message, usually of a romantic nature. Here was a scheme that was to prove an invaluable asset to gold-smiths, and its use in jewellery is widespread. It is especially important in helping us understand the significance of the tiara as a symbol of married love.

When an emblematic flower is incorporated into the design of a tiara set with a particular conjunction of precious stones, the combination of the two conveys a powerful message of love (for example, Plates 16–18).

Many tiaras are set with rubies and diamonds to evoke enduring passion, and a wreath of oak entirely set with turquoise stands for the invincibility of true love. When Queen Elizabeth the Queen Mother (then Lady Elizabeth Bowes-Lyon) married in 1923, her father gave her a tiara in the form of a garland of wild roses, for every aspect of love, set with rose-cut diamonds for eternity (Plate 12, opposite).

The Language of Flowers

Acorn – Fecundity
Daisy – Innocence
Forget-me-not – True Love
Ivy – Marriage
Laurel – Triumph of Love
Mistletoe – A Kiss
Oak – Invincibility and Strength
Rose – Every Aspect of Love
Thistle Flower – The Pleasure and
   Pain of Love
Pansy – Think of the Giver

The Lore of the Lapidary

Amethyst – Devotion
Diamond – Forever
Emerald – Hope
Moonstone – Innocence
Pearl – Love
Ruby – Passion
Turquoise – Remembrance and
   True Love

12 The tiara of wild roses set with rose-cut diamonds given by the 14th Earl of Strathmore to his daughter, Lady Elizabeth Bowes-Lyon (Queen Elizabeth the Queen Mother), when she married the Duke of York (King George VI) on 26 April 1923. In the language of flowers, the wild rose represents love in all its aspects, whether joyful or painful. In giving this jewel to a bride the Earl was following a very ancient tradition. By Gracious Permission of Her Majesty Queen Elizabeth the Queen Mother.

Many old families uphold a long-standing tradition by which the bride wears a particular family tiara. In doing so, she marks her transition from one domestic role to another, and she is not likely to have use of it again. Its place will be taken by gifts from her husband, or perhaps his ancestral jewels will be re-set specifically for her use. When, in the summer of 1981, Lady Diana Spencer married the Prince of Wales in St Paul's Cathedral, it came as no surprise that she chose to wear the Spencer family tiara. Although few will have forgotten her dramatic dress, designed for her by David and Elizabeth Emanuel, the scintillation of the Spencer tiara, mounted in gold in the form of stylized flowers entirely decorated with diamonds in silver settings, left an indelible impression on the millions watching on television all over the world.

Even the simplest of gem-set tiaras can generate a similar sense of excitement at a wedding, as is testified by Lucy Graham Smith's description of Pamela Wyndham immediately after her marriage to the first Baron Glenconnor in 1895: 'Coming down the aisle after the service she had thrown her veil back and just showed the circlet of brilliants round the small domed head… she was like a thing inspired… I have never seen a bride so lovely.' Even today, when both religion and the institution of marriage are in perilous decline, the tiara continues to exert its influence on us all, albeit subliminally. For marriage at least, it remains as significant today as it was in deepest antiquity.

13 *(opposite)* A tiara in the form of conventionalized foliage set with turquoise and diamonds, given to Princess Mary as a wedding present by her parents, the Duke and Duchess of Teck, when she married the Duke of York in 1893. The gift of this tiara was particularly appropriate for such an occasion, as the conjunction of these two stones signifies enduring love.
Their Royal Highnesses the Duke and Duchess of Gloucester.

14 Her Royal Highness Princess Alice, Duchess of Gloucester, photographed by Cecil Beaton wearing the turquoise and diamond tiara, with matching necklace, brooch and earrings.
Victoria and Albert Museum Picture Library.

15 *(below)* A design for a diadem of carnations tied with a lovers' knot, c.1890, by E. Wolff & Co., who were manufacturers to Garrard. In the language of flowers, the pink carnation stands for a woman's love. E. Wolfe & Co.

16 *(above)* A gold circlet, probably intended for a bride, in the form of lilies made of white enamel interspersed with pearl drops and diamonds. The frame of the jewel is overlaid with stylized forget-me-not flowers set with turquoise, diamonds and rubies. This jewel is a potent emblem of love. The lily is symbolic of purity, the forget-me-not, represented by the turquoise, stands for true love, the conjunction of the diamond and the pearl signifies everlasting love, and the ruby and the diamond the hope of enduring passion. Probably French, c.1870. Fred Leighton, New York.

15207
15212
1521
15216
30
15218

17 *(below)* A design for a tiara
arranged as two ears of wheat,
by the jewellery workmaster
Holmström for Fabergé, 1909.
In the language of flowers the ear
of wheat stands for fertility and
wealth, a most welcome blessing
for a bride, here subtly endorsed
by the presence of diamonds.
Wartski, London.

18 *(above)* A seed pearl diadem
arranged as a garland of wild
roses. As with the Strathmore tiara
(Plate 12), this jewel is emblematic
of the pleasure and pain of love,
but here the message is reinforced
by the presence of pearls, which
are born of the sea like Venus
herself and rank among her
familiars. In conjunction with the
rose, the pearls make the symbolic
significance of this charming tiara
doubly powerful. Nicholas and
Sharon Wood.

1909 г.

Diadема

54 брил. 2 25/руу ; 144 розы à' ту

19, 20 *(left)* Princess Elizabeth on her wedding day, 20 November 1947. She is wearing the Russian fringe tiara *(below left)* that was made for Queen Mary in 1919, and is said to contain diamonds that belonged to George III. Perhaps for this reason it is often worn by royal brides. The tiara is made of brilliant diamonds mounted in gold and set in silver. Despite its name, the Russian fringe tiara, or '*tiare russe*', was especially popular in England, and hundreds, if not thousands, were made. Most can be detached from their frames and worn as necklaces. The Queen has worn this jewel as both. Photograph by Baron, Camera Press, London. Tiara photograph: © Reserved/The Royal Collection.

21 *(opposite)* A diamond tiara in the form of wild roses and carnations. The flowers are mounted *en tremblant* and are animated by the slightest movement of the head. Composed of two early 19th-century jewels, it is said to have belonged to Lady Caroline Lamb. The tiara was rearranged in the late 19th century. The flowers chosen for the design, which stand for a woman's true love, are curiously appropriate for Lady Caroline, whose life was blighted by her disastrous affair with Lord Byron. Private Collection.

22 *(right)* A design for a tiara in the form of the wings of love, by E. Wolff & Co., 1906. Tiaras such as this were popular at the turn of the century and were probably inspired by the amuletic winged globe of Ancient Egypt. However, this highly successful design quickly acquired a more modern interpretation, and came to stand for the wings of love. E. Wolfe & Co., London.

23 *(below)* A small diadem of diamonds arranged as a radiant sunburst. The centre can be removed and worn as a brooch. French, c.1900. Wartski, London.

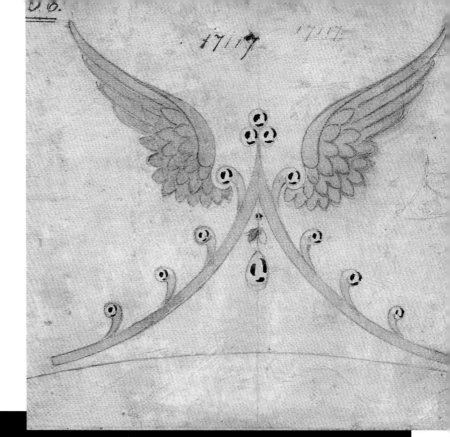

24 A tiara in the form of five stars supported on a gallery of stylized foliage. A highly successful tiara type, these jewels invite comparison between starshine and the scintillation of the diamond. The inclusion of stars may also allude to Shakespeare's Sonnet 116, in which he describes love as 'the star to every wandering bark'. Private Collection.

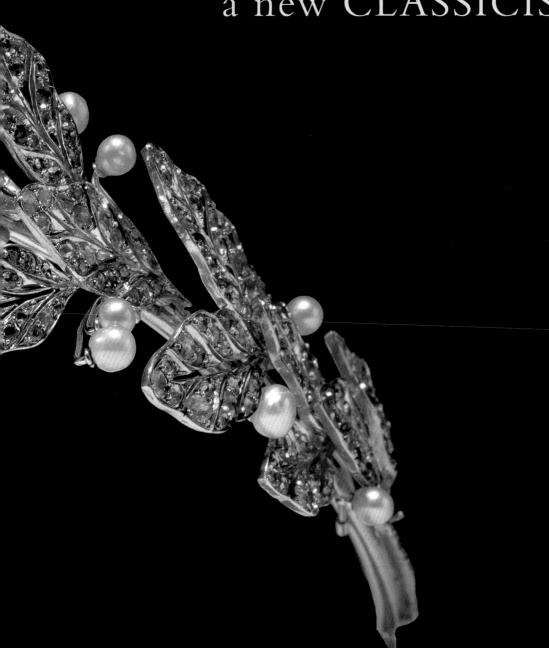

a new CLASSICISM

AFTER centuries spent languishing in relative obscurity, the tiara experienced a dramatic revival during the latter years of the 18th century. There are two main reasons for this, the first being the rise of neo-classicism. This movement is often seen mainly as a reaction to the excesses of rococo and baroque, but its advent also coincided with a growing cultural awareness of antique artefacts that had survived from the days of the ancient Mediterranean civilizations. Fresh archaeological discoveries inspired all manner of decorative artists and craftsmen, including goldsmiths and jewellers, with new ideas and new enthusiasm. Early discoveries of gold ornaments in the cemeteries of Etruria, and at the Roman sites of Pompeii and Herculaneum, had revealed that the Ancients were not only master architects and sculptors but brilliant metalworkers, too. In England, the arrival of the Elgin Marbles in 1804 provoked a wave of passionate admiration for all things classical. They affected Keats so profoundly that he described the sensation he experienced as a 'dizzy pain'.

25 Empress Josephine, painted in 1808 by baron François Gérard. She is wearing her coronation robes and an immensely valuable parure of emeralds and pearls from her personal collection. Her tiara is worn low on her forehead, and her hair is secured with a comb decorated with pearls. Château de Fontainebleau © photo RMN.

In France, another event took place that year that was to affect the course of fashion all over the continent. Napoleon Bonaparte crowned himself Emperor. Lacking the dynastic credentials of his predecessors, the Bourbons, he was anxious to establish a new decorative scheme that would endorse his imperial status. Nothing suited his needs better than to emulate the style of Imperial Rome. At his coronation he and his Empress, Josephine, were robed '*à la romaine*'. She and her attendant ladies were decked in sumptuous jewellery based on classical prototypes, and on each head blazed a different gem-set wreath or diadem. Some of these were set with

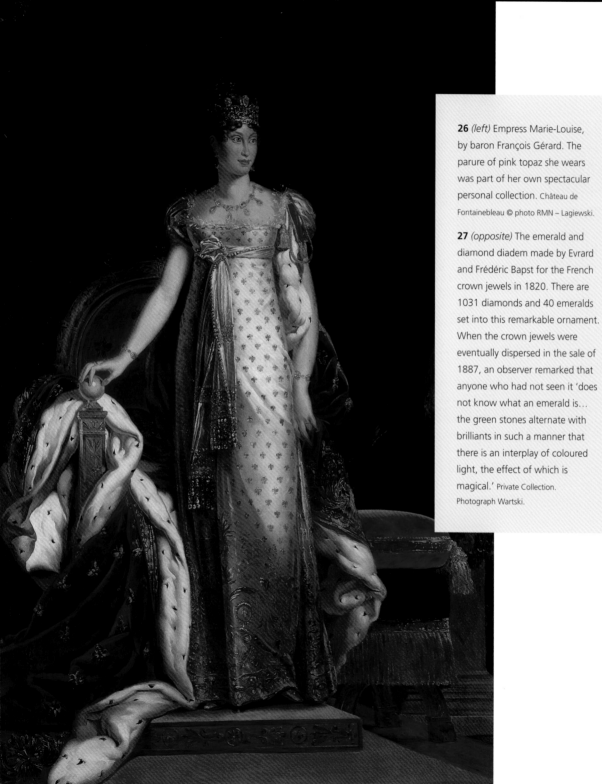

26 *(left)* Empress Marie-Louise, by baron François Gérard. The parure of pink topaz she wears was part of her own spectacular personal collection. Château de Fontainebleau © photo RMN – Lagiewski.

27 *(opposite)* The emerald and diamond diadem made by Evrard and Frédéric Bapst for the French crown jewels in 1820. There are 1031 diamonds and 40 emeralds set into this remarkable ornament. When the crown jewels were eventually dispersed in the sale of 1887, an observer remarked that anyone who had not seen it 'does not know what an emerald is… the green stones alternate with brilliants in such a manner that there is an interplay of coloured light, the effect of which is magical.' Private Collection. Photograph Wartski.

antique cameos that were intended to make another reference to a remote, yet powerful and, above all, dependable past.

Clearly the new fashion for classicism had swept away previous styles, and the prejudices that had suppressed the revival of the tiara up to this point. It was now free to take its place as a fashionable part of modern dress, and was adopted by ladies of society with genuine enthusiasm and commitment. Although the uncertain politics that blighted France during the 19th century meant that the tiara was to swing in and out of favour there, the court society of other European nations was now afforded the opportunity to wear some of the most beautiful head ornaments ever created.

28, 29, 30 A magnificent tiara and comb set with pink spinels and diamonds, made for the young widow of Prince Peter Ivanovitch Bagration, the Russian beauty Princess Catherine (1783–1857). The Princess, who was related to both Catherine I and Elizabeth I of Russia, probably owned several other parures of coloured stones. This particular example, however, is quite splendid, and is a rare survival of a type of tiara, made with matching comb, that was popular at the court of Napoleon Bonaparte. The necklace and earrings are of a later date, made for one of the Princess's descendants in the 1870s, but are undoubtedly of Russian manufacture. The suite of jewellery was purchased by the 6th and present Duke of Westminster at the time of his marriage to Natalia Phillips in 1978. Their Graces the Duke and Duchess of Westminster.

31 A wreath of laurel leaves and berries cleverly suggested by pale emeralds and grey pearls. The laurel wreath, much favoured in antiquity, was revived during the First Empire and remained popular until the early 20th century. This example is probably English and dates from about 1900. Private Collection. Photograph Wartski.

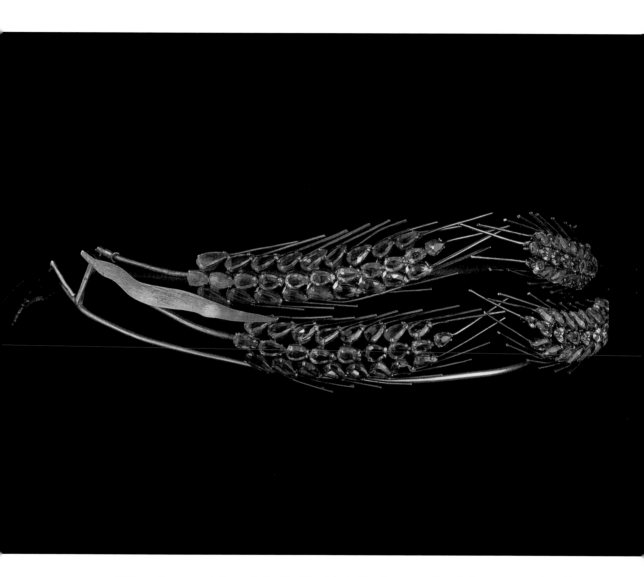

32 A wreath composed of ears of wheat in gilt metal set with yellow pastes. Ears of wheat were a popular subject for gold wreaths in Ancient Greece, and this charming example probably derives from a prototype of that period. English, c. 1830. Private Collection. Photograph Wartski.

at COURT

33, 34 This portrait of the young Queen Victoria was painted by Franz Winterhalter in 1842. It is thought that the choice of dress and the unconventional placing of the sapphire and diamond tiara on her head were made at Prince Albert's instigation. Perhaps he intended the painting to evoke the portrait of Queen Henrietta Maria after Van Dyck (now in the National Portrait Gallery, London). The tiara *(opposite)* was designed by the Prince and made in 1842 by Joseph Kitching at a cost of £415. Its intimate scale and subdued colours allowed her to wear it over her white widow's cap when, in 1866, she opened Parliament for the first time since Albert's death five years before. Royal Collection © 2001, Her Majesty Queen Elizabeth II. Tiara: The Earl and Countess of Harewood.

IN England, the monarchy enjoyed much greater security than many of the other European royal families during the 19th century, and such stability allowed the tiara, an important symbol of power and rank, to be enthusiastically embraced. The tastes and customs at court had a huge influence on the culture and fashion of the time, and the Queen and the Prince Consort were both passionate about jewellery. The climate was right for the tiara to flourish.

Queen Victoria was just nineteen when she came to the throne in 1837. Few who saw her remained unmoved by her youthful beauty, and many artists were asked to paint her portrait. Most of them chose to represent her sovereignty with the aid of her magnificent tiaras, of which she had several. Even before she was married the Queen had made use of a valuable diamond diadem for that purpose, at court, at numerous dances and even when she visited the theatre in Covent Garden. In the absence of photography the public had little notion of the sovereign's appearance, and this majestic jewel must have gone a long way towards identifying this tiny young girl as Queen.

When she married her cousin, Prince Albert of Saxe-Coburg-Gotha, in 1840, her collection of jewellery became the focus of serious attention for them both (for example, Plate 35). She wrote in her journal: 'My dear Albert has such good taste and arranges everything for me about my jewellery.' At least three of her tiaras were made up under his direction (Plate 34); the Oriental Circlet (Plate 37) was a special favourite, and she enjoyed wearing it with fresh waterlilies in her hair.

After Albert's death in 1861 the Queen retreated into a state of perpetual mourning, and her splendid tiaras set with coloured gemstones were abandoned in favour of a white widow's cap. The responsibility for court entertainment

fell to the Prince of Wales and his beautiful wife Alexandra, who was a Danish princess. He, like his father before him, was fascinated by every aspect of dress and was a stickler for detail. The wearing of tiaras at court was something on which he was insistent and the failure to do so would bring a stinging rebuke. On one occasion Consuelo, Duchess of Marlborough, a guest at a dinner in honour of the Prince and Princess, had not had time to retrieve her tiara from the bank before the evening began. She had resorted to a diamond crescent for her hair, but this did not satisfy the Prince, who asked: 'The Princess has taken the trouble to wear a tiara, why have you not done so?'

By the time Edward VII came to the throne in 1901, colonial and industrial expansion had resulted in great prosperity and a widening of nobility and society. It was at this time that the tiara was in greatest demand. Thousands were made in London, and in Paris the famous firms of Cartier, Boucheron and Chaumet were also busy satisfying the demands of the newly ennobled. In St Petersburg it was Fabergé who topped a list of highly gifted goldsmiths and jewellers. Improvements in travel and communications meant that their wares were now attracting custom from as far away as America, and if long journeys were likely to discourage a wealthy international clientele, then the jewellers were prepared to go to them.

By 1900, following the exchange of huge dowries for titles, there were fifty American ladies in the British peerage. Their independent means allowed them to shield themselves from snobbery behind the glittering bastions of the finest modern jewellery. Some of this was set in pure white platinum, which

Olga.
Paris 1929.

36 A photograph of Princess Olga, known after her marriage as Princess Paul of Yugoslavia, taken in 1929. Olga is seen here wearing an impressive Art Deco-style diamond bracelet, two strings of valuable pearls, a pearl ring and a large and impressive diamond-set diadem by Cartier. Such a show of valuable jewellery was appropriate because she was a princess, but it also bears poignant testimony to her status as a descendant of Tsar Alexander II – she was described by 'Chips' Channon as 'very royal'. Olga was one of the last princesses to have played with the children of Tsar Nicholas II. His Royal Highness Prince Alexander of Yugoslavia.

contrasted with the darker silver and gold settings that the American women tended to dislike.

After a reign of just nine years King Edward died, and the following year his son was crowned King George V. The new Queen, Mary, had a unique regal poise and dignity that she endorsed with the finest gem-set jewellery, including a number of splendid tiaras. Some she had inherited, but several new diadems were made especially for her use, such as the magnificent tiara that Garrard made for her to wear at her husband's coronation as Emperor of India in December 1911. The King considered it her 'best tiara'. Such was the royal regard for the tiara that it was deemed mandatory on other, more intimate occasions. Lady Cynthia Colville recorded that 'Almost every night the King and Queen dined alone or with their children in the private apartments. The King wore a tail coat and the Garter and The Queen always put on a tiara for dinner.'

Queen Mary was a descendant of King George III, and mindful of this, she took a keen interest in objects of royal provenance. She was always pleased to acquire them, and after the Russian Revolution the opportunity arose for her to buy the pearl and diamond tiara that had belonged to the Grand Duchess Vladimir. The Duchess's daughter, Princess Nicholas of Greece, had inherited it, and when she decided to sell, it was Queen Mary who saved the jewel from probable obscurity. It was later adapted so that its pearls could be interchanged with a magnificent collection of emerald drops. Even towards the end of her life Queen Mary's enthusiasm for precious and beautiful things remained undiminished, and of course the finest jewellery took pride of place in her collections. Sir Osbert Sitwell, a guest at Badminton where Queen Mary was staying during the Second World War, recorded his impression of her when she appeared at dinner, covered in diamonds, 'magnificent – blazing, sparkling'. A fellow guest remarked: 'I wonder if you realise it but when this old lady is gone, you'll never see anything like this, or her, again!'

George V died in 1936, and the new king, Edward VIII, abdicated on 10 December 1936, before his coronation could take place. When his brother was crowned King George VI, on 12 May 1937, Queen Mary recorded that she 'felt very sad' at parting with the jewellery she had looked after since 1910. Now it was for the use of the new Queen, Elizabeth. Among its treasures were several historic tiaras, including the Delhi Durbar tiara, the tiara of crescents which

37, 38 The Oriental Circlet, originally designed in 1853. Prince Albert is believed to have been closely involved in the concept of this remarkable jewel, which was originally set with opals. Queen Alexandra had these replaced with rubies in 1902. Queen Elizabeth the Queen Mother wore it in 1948 when she was photographed *(right)* by Cecil Beaton, who may well have had Winterhalter's portraits of Queen Victoria in mind when he asked her to pose in this way. Victoria and Albert Museum Picture Library. Tiara photograph by Gracious Permission of Her Majesty Queen Elizabeth the Queen Mother.

had once been worn by Queen Mary's mother, Princess Mary Adelaide of Teck, the Regal Circlet of George IV, and the Oriental Circlet (Plate 37). In 1942 Queen Elizabeth was bequeathed a magnificent collection of jewellery by the Hon. Mrs Greville, which included a neo-classical tiara made by Boucheron in January 1921, and this has become one of her special favourites.

Not all Queen Elizabeth's jewellery was inherited. She was to receive a number of magnificent jewels that had been purchased specifically for her. The firm of Cartier had been a particular favourite of the King. As a result Queen Elizabeth was given a multigem bandeau that converts to bracelets, a diamond tiara in the Art Deco taste, and an aquamarine and diamond tiara that had been made by the now famous French firm. These made a striking contrast to the more traditional tiara set in silver and gold that her father, the Earl of Strathmore, had given her when she married in 1923 (Plate 12).

The present Queen owns a dramatic collection of jewellery, and amongst it is a number of fine tiaras, including the Regal Circlet and the Grand Duchess Vladimir's tiara. Two others were made to Queen Mary's order, the Cambridge Lovers' Knot tiara in November 1913, and the Russian fringe tiara in 1919. When she married, the Queen was given a diamond tiara that was originally Queen Mary's own wedding present from the Girls of Great Britain and Ireland. This particular tiara remains one of Her Majesty's favourites. The Queen has also commissioned new tiaras, and these are set with aquamarines, sapphires and diamonds, and rubies and diamonds.

39 A tiara in the form of stylized daisy leaves and flowers. Each flower or bud is suggested by a pale yellow diamond. It was ordered by the Georgian Princess Abamalek on 10 December 1907 from Boucheron, and was made by the outworker Basset. The diamond rivière necklace that runs along the bottom of the jewel is a later addition, apparently made by Princess Paul of Yugoslavia. Even before her marriage to Prince Paul she ranked highly in royal circles as she was the granddaughter of King George I of Greece. Private Collection.

The Cartier Art Deco style tiara has now passed to Princess Margaret and is part of a distinguished group of historic jewels in Her Royal Highness's collection, which includes the diadem in the form of stylized lotus leaves given by Queen Mary to Queen Elizabeth the Queen Mother. There is also a turquoise and diamond tiara decorated with emblems of love, which is a miracle of the gem-setter's art. It is only exceeded in splendour by the late 19th-century tiara made by Garrard which was purchased in celebration of Her Royal Highness's marriage in 1960. Historic tiaras now belong to other members of the Royal Family. Those that deserve special mention are the Cartier aquamarine and

diamond tiara, and the Greek key pattern tiara that has passed to the Princess Royal (Plate 47). There are two splendid tiaras that belonged to Princess Marina in the collection of Prince and Princess Michael of Kent. Their Royal Highnesses the Duke and Duchess of Gloucester have Queen Mary's honeysuckle tiara made by Garrard and the extraordinary pearl, sapphire and diamond tiara which has been passed down to them from Queen Victoria's granddaughter, Princess Marie Louise.

During the reigns of King Edward VII, George V and King George VI one of the most spectacular events of the royal calendar was Their Majesty's Courts, at which the season's debutantes, as well as a variety of foreign diplomats, would be presented to the King and Queen. It was a spectacle of great splendour focused upon Their Majesty's thrones, where the royal couple stood, in full court dress, to receive the seemingly endless queue of young ladies either on the brink of entering society or being presented at court following their marriage. Confusion over the identity of the candidates was avoided when King Edward VII made it mandatory for debutantes to wear three ostrich feathers in their hair. A senior lady who was, in most instances, the debutante's mother, always made the presentation. These ladies were obliged to wear a gem-set tiara, as was the candidate, if she were married. The sight must have been quite unforgettable. Sadly this delightful custom, like so many formal occasions that called for a jewelled head-dress, is now practically obsolete.

40 *Going to Court*, by James Hayllar, 1863. This painting of two women, evidently on their way to Court for presentation to the Sovereign, tells a more complicated story than first appears. The diamond-set diadems indicate that both are married, and it is likely that the younger of the two is to be presented by her mother as a new bride. The women are insulated from the world outside not only by their carriage but also by their status and its trappings – valuable silks, pearls and diamond-set jewellery. Private Collection. Photograph Christopher Wood.

41 The famous amethysts given by Tsar Alexander I to Lady Londonderry in 1821, which were later mounted in diamond-set clusters to form a long stomacher and a tiara. The best Russian amethysts come from Siberian mines, which were then owned by the Tsar. They are said to be the finest in the world because of the red and blue highlights seen in the deep purple body colour of the stones. Lady Londonderry was charmed by the amorous attentions of the Tsar and by the precious stones he heaped upon her, but she managed to end the love affair 'innocent of guilt'. The stones are here shown against the original design for the tiara by E. Wolff & Co., which is dated August 1916. The conversion to a tiara was probably made to mark the succession of the 7th Marquess on 8 February 1915. The Most Hon. The Marquess of Londonderry and E. Wolfe & Co.

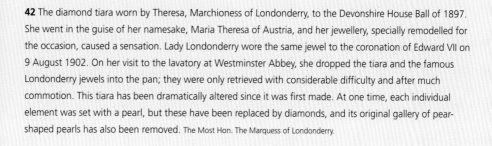

42 The diamond tiara worn by Theresa, Marchioness of Londonderry, to the Devonshire House Ball of 1897. She went in the guise of her namesake, Maria Theresa of Austria, and her jewellery, specially remodelled for the occasion, caused a sensation. Lady Londonderry wore the same jewel to the coronation of Edward VII on 9 August 1902. On her visit to the lavatory at Westminster Abbey, she dropped the tiara and the famous Londonderry jewels into the pan; they were only retrieved with considerable difficulty and after much commotion. This tiara has been dramatically altered since it was first made. At one time, each individual element was set with a pearl, but these have been replaced by diamonds, and its original gallery of pear-shaped pearls has also been removed. The Most Hon. The Marquess of Londonderry.

43 Princess Marina of Greece arriving at Westminster Abbey for her wedding to the Duke of Kent on 29 November 1934. She is wearing the diamond fringe tiara given to her as a wedding present from the City of London. This remarkable photograph comes from Queen Mary's album and is captioned in her own hand. The Royal Archives © Her Majesty Queen Elizabeth II.

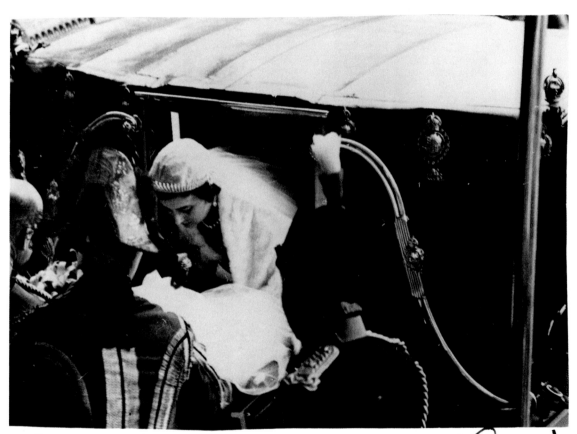

44 *(above) Princess Marina's diamond fringe tiara, English, c.1890. This type of tiara, which can often be converted into a necklace, is called a 'Russian fringe' because the highly successful design is said to derive from Russian prototypes. Literally thousands were made at the end of the 19th and beginning of the 20th centuries.*
The choice of this jewel as a wedding present may well have been a subtle compliment to the Princess's Russian ancestry. Their Royal Highnesses the Prince and Princess Michael of Kent.

45 *(opposite)* A diamond tiara arranged as an alternating fringe of graduated volutes, each surmounted by a pearl. Probably English, *c.*1900. This jewel was a favourite of Princess Marina, Duchess of Kent, who enjoyed wearing it when she was photographed or sat for portraits. It is now worn by Her Royal Highness Princess Michael of Kent, and its height has been increased by the addition of a string of pearls to its base. Their Royal Highnesses the Prince and Princess Michael of Kent.

46 *(right)* A portrait of Princess Marina, Duchess of Kent, by Simon Elwes, *c.*1950. The beautiful princess is wearing the pearl and diamond tiara with a diamond rivière necklace, girandole earrings and a large diamond-set bow at her waist. Their Royal Highnesses the Prince and Princess Michael of Kent.

47 *(opposite)* A platinum tiara in the form of a Greek key pattern interspaced with honeysuckles and triumphal laurels. French, c.1900. This charming diadem once belonged to Princess Andrew of Greece, mother of the Duke of Edinburgh. It is French and bears a close similarity to another made by Cartier at this time. Her Royal Highness, the Princess Royal.

48 *(right)* The photograph of the Princess Royal taken by John Swannell to celebrate her 50th birthday in August 2000. The Greek key pattern tiara is a particular favourite of the Princess, not only because it belonged to her grandmother, but also because its simple, uncluttered lines are curiously contemporary. Camera Press, London.

a return to the ANTIQUE

IN the mid-19th century, the creative momentum behind decorative art in Europe started to falter. Designers appeared to be suffering from a lack of vision – it was almost as if they had lost confidence in their ability to conceive anything truly original. It seemed that the only course left open to them was to seek inspiration from sources that were far removed both in time and place from the industrialized world; only by harking back to the work of their classical predecessors, or by following the example of master craftsmen from other continents and cultures, could they be assured the aesthetic credentials they felt were so evidently lacking in themselves. It is difficult to understand why this mood should have prevailed in a society where there had been so many spectacular advances; perhaps it was partly to do with the social unrest and political uncertainty that blighted the continent through-out the century, and was eventually to culminate in the Great War. For countries such as Russia, which needed to stabilize and reinforce its national identity, and Italy, which needed to reinvent its own, the past held the key.

There was certainly no shortage of source material for artists to draw upon. To the fascination of everyone, archaeological discoveries were being made at a rate hitherto unknown, and in many different parts of the world. Communications net-works had been vastly improved, and the increased prosperity of the middle classes, together with imperialist links with Africa, Asia and the Indian subcontinent, had encouraged travel. And for those who were unable to see ancient treasures in their original context, there were illustrated publications

49 A gold tiara by Carlo Giuliano supporting a stylized wreath of banded agate laurel leaves and pearl berries; the front of the jewel takes the form of a rosette of similarly carved petals centring on a single pearl. London, c.1860. Although this tiara would have been suitable for mourning, its black and white colour-scheme, inspired by Renaissance prototypes, was also highly fashionable at the time. Private Collection.

documenting these inspiring finds. The international network of museums we take so much for granted today was also bringing together fascinating collections of classical antiquities at that time, and exhibiting them alongside Ancient Egyptian, Far Eastern and ethnic works of art. Jewellery designers were therefore able to draw on all manner of exotic sources, which they could reinterpret and incorporate with great flair into contemporary tiaras (Plate 56).

In the late 1840s the goldsmith and antiques dealer Fortunato Pio Castellani founded the School of Italian Archaeological Jewellery in Rome, with the specific intention of making pastiches. These were self-consciously modern jewels made in homage to ancient prototypes, and were designed to be worn by modern women. Naturally the gold wreaths and diadems popular in antiquity

were, for their elegance and dramatic effect, particularly popular with Castellani and his patrons (Plate 55). His premises by the Trevi Fountain were a favourite destination on the Grand Tour, and ladies of fashion proudly returned to England with all manner of interesting jewellery, including tiaras. Popular with followers of the Aesthetic Movement, these head ornaments looked strangely incongruous in cold and foggy London.

Nonetheless the fashion for revivalist jewellery took a firm hold in the capital, and in 1860 Alessandro Castellani established a branch there. Its first manager was a Neapolitan by the name of Carlo Giuliano, who went on to found a business under his own name in 1874, widening the focus of inspiration to include the Renaissance style (Plate 49). Giuliano's shop at 115 Piccadilly was popular with a small but discriminating clientele which included a number of prominent British artists. In fact it may well have been Sir Edward Burne-Jones who inspired Giuliano to make a series of jewels of almost Pre-Raphaelite intensity and charm.

Although Archaeological jewellery was popular in Russia, as in the rest of Europe, Fabergé and his competitors in St Petersburg and Moscow preferred to focus their attention on ornaments of purely Russian ancestry, and in particular the kokoshnik. This head-dress had been part of traditional folk costume since remotest antiquity (see page 12), but during the 19th century its patriotic associations strengthened its appeal at a time when foreign influence was felt to be undermining national identity. The word 'kokoshnik' literally means 'cockscomb', and describes the undulating line that characterizes most of these head ornaments. Generally they were made of a stiff card covered with velvet, to which glittering ornaments were attached. All that was necessary for the

50 *A Personification of Russia*, a bronze portrait bust by Mikail Afanasievitch Chijov, *c.*1880. The young Russian beauty here portrayed is wearing a cap of freshwater pearls surmounted by a traditional kokoshnik. This ancient folk head-dress was the prototype for many gem-set tiaras made not only in Russia but also in London, Paris and New York. Sotheby's.

goldsmith to do was to wave his magic wand over these humble head-dresses to transmute them into one of the noblest forms of jewellery. Intrinsically valuable kokoshniks were traditionally worn at court, but the style was given fresh impetus by a series of palace balls given in anticipation of the Romanov tercentenary in 1913. Keen to feel a part of this, Russians living abroad chose to wear jewelled kokoshniks, and the style was soon taken up by jewellers in France, London and even as far away as New York. The tragic events that followed the Revolution of 1917 put a stop to the work of the jewellers in St Petersburg and Moscow, but in Paris Cartier was to continue making jewelled kokoshniks for another decade.

A revival of the neo-classical fashions of 18th-century France was also enjoying popularity at this time. They offered a lighter, more easily assimilated alternative, and were much admired in royal and aristocratic circles. The jewellery houses were quick to exploit the new trend, and Fabergé, Cartier, Boucheron and even Tiffany all made diamond jewellery mounted in platinum in the Louis XVI style. Typically it incorporated amatory trophies with trails of roses and forget-me-nots, which earned it the name 'garland style'.

By 1900 the majority of these revivalist styles were in recession. A movement that spurned all historicism had taken their place. It was called Art Nouveau.

51 *(left)* A photograph of the Tsarina Alexandra Feodorovna, wife of Nicholas II, signed, and dated 1899. She is wearing the fringe tiara from the crown jewels against a velvet kokoshnik. Around her neck is the valuable necklace of pearls and pearl drops purchased from Fabergé by her father-in-law as a wedding present. Of the vast collection of jewellery that was at the Tsarina's disposal, she loved her pearls the best. Wartski, London.

52 *(opposite)* A tiara in the form of a traditional blue velvet kokoshnik actually made of platinum and plique-à-jour enamel overlaid with diamond-set forget-me-not flowers, emblematic of true love. Purchased by the 2nd Duke of Westminster at Chaumet on 29 September 1911 for £375. It is set with 280 brilliant-cut diamonds and 314 rose-cut diamonds. Their Graces the Duke and Duchess of Westminster.

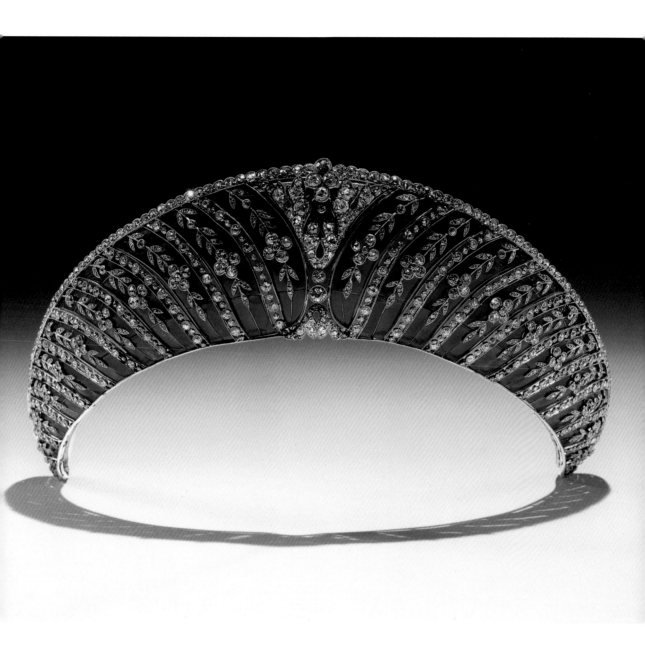

53 *(opposite)* The Pakenham tiara, arranged as a circlet of honeysuckle motifs decorated with diamonds set in silver and mounted in gold. The individual elements are removable and can be used as brooches or dress ornaments. It may have been made for the widow of the 1st Baron Longford, who was elevated to the Irish title of Countess nine years after her husband's death in 1776.
Private Collection.

54 *(below)* A large Siberian amethyst mounted as a jewel with diamond-set honeysuckle motifs, c.1810. At a later date it was made the centre of this amethyst and diamond tiara in the form of vine leaves that are a witty allusion to the purple stones. The word 'amethyst' derives from the Greek *amethustos*, literally meaning 'not drunken', referring to the belief that an amethyst placed in a glass of wine would allow one to drink without fear of intoxication. In the lore of the ancient lapidaries, the amethyst also stood for devotion in love. The Most Hon. the Marquess of Tavistock. Photograph Wartski.

56 *(right)* A gold tiara made to resemble the Ancient Egyptian amuletic winged globe, by Carlo and Arthur Giuliano, London, c.1900. Set with brilliant diamonds and decorated with green enamel, the globe is represented with a star ruby. Despite its form, the influence of Ancient Egyptian art is only slightly evident in this dramatic jewel. Its origins seem more Pre-Raphaelite than ancient, and its eccentricity is typically English. Private Collection.

55 *(below)* A gold diadem fashioned in the form of three parallel twisted ribbons secured with a central knot of Hercules and decorated with enamel and a single cabochon hessonite garnet, c.1895. This jewel is based directly on a diadem from Melos, made in the 3rd century BC, that was once in the Castellani collection and acquired by the British Museum in 1872. This is a late example of the Archaeological style of jewellery fashionable in the 1860s. It may have been made for one of the many costume pageants that were popular at the turn of the century. Private Collection.

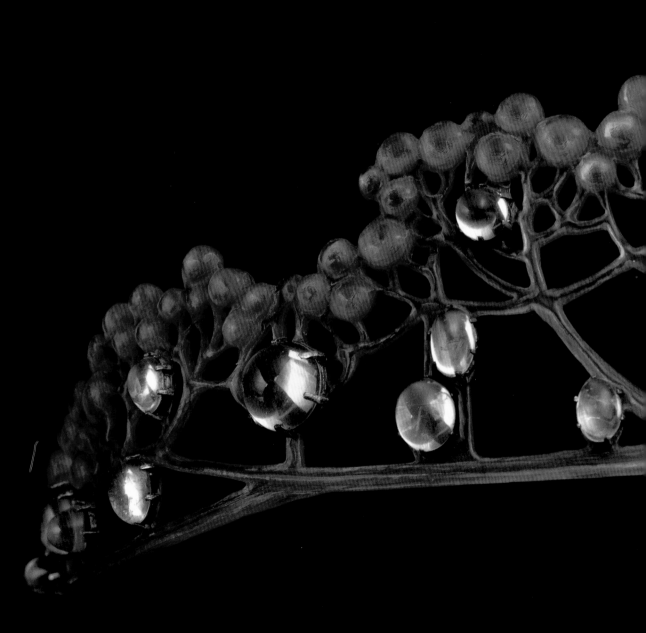

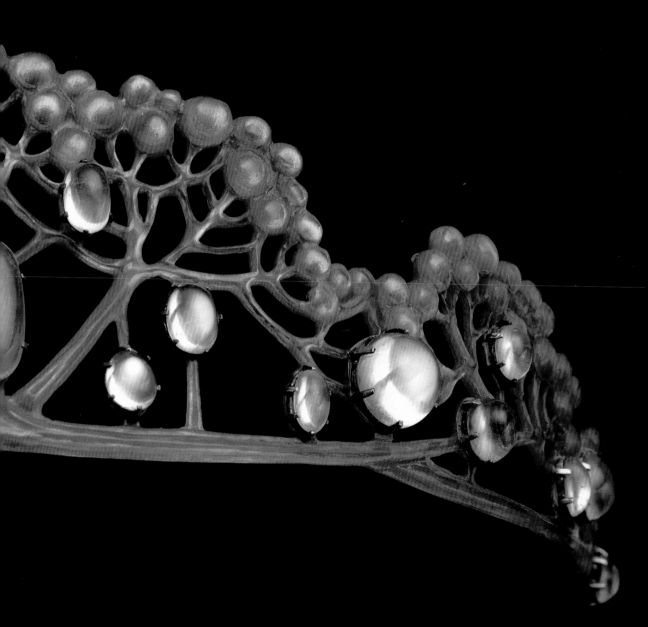

a WORK of ART

THE publicity that surrounded the International Exhibitions and Salons held at the turn of the century brought heavy pressure to bear on the decorative artists, whatever their specialization. They were constantly expected to excel themselves in craftsmanship, novelty and eccentricity of design. Jewellers were no exception, and the majority of them were quick to recognize the dramatic potential of the tiara. Before long it was to break through the constraints of practicality and realize its potential as a work of art in its own right. Designers working in the Arts and Crafts tradition were to make some highly imaginative head ornaments, but the most remarkable of all were the creations of the Art Nouveau jewellers.

The Arts and Crafts movement first evolved as a reaction against the 'tyranny' of industrialism on everyday life, and in jewellery design this meant rejecting mass production and proclaiming the virtues of the hand-made. Its creeds were rooted in the theories of Augustus Welby Pugin, John Ruskin and William Morris, and it also espoused the belief that art should be nationalistic, a popular sentiment in many European countries at the time. The crusade for 'English Art for England' culminated in the return to medievalism: artists in the Middle Ages, as in the Renaissance, were involved in every aspect of their work, and this included goldsmith's work and jewellery.

Customers who despaired of the 'tastelessness and vulgarity' of the jewellery now emerging from the factories of Birmingham and the East End looked to London's specialist art jewellers to provide them with work of the quality that was so lamentably lacking elsewhere. The firms of Giuliano, Robert Philips and Child and Child guaranteed real craftsmanship as well as design sources that had sufficient integrity to attract the most particular clientele, some of

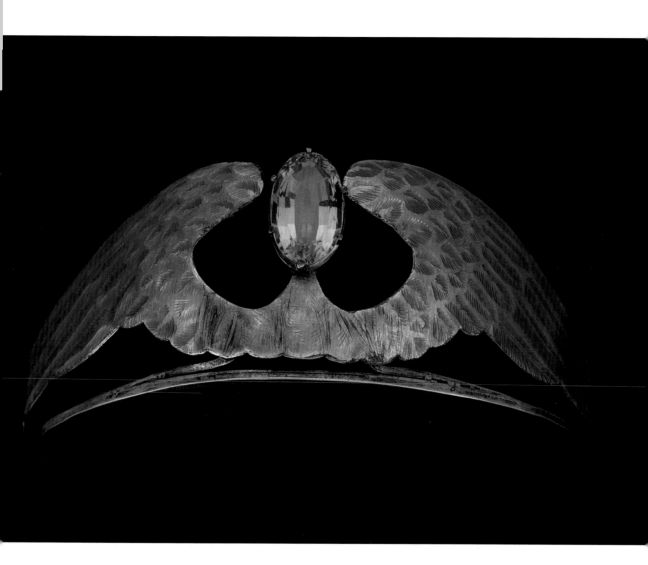

57 A diadem in the form of an amuletic winged globe set centrally with a citrine, by Child and Child, c.1900. Harold and Walter Child ran a business in South Kensington that was popular not only with the extended family of Queen Victoria but also with the artistic community of London, and could name among its patrons William Holman Hunt, Sir Edward Burne-Jones and Sir Edwin Lutyens. Child and Child's jewellery is characterized by vibrantly coloured enamel-work rather than by valuable precious stones. Tadema Gallery, London.

them royal or aristocratic, others of the newly lauded artistic elite. Of the individual jewellers who were able to live up to these exacting standards, among the most gifted were Frederick Partridge (1877–1942) and Henry Wilson (1864–1934). Wilson was trained as an architect but by 1890 had taken up goldsmith's work, and this had soon begun to dominate his career. He had established a workshop by the mid-1890s, and from it emerged some of the most hauntingly beautiful tiaras ever made in England. His work is seldom signed, but can be recognized by his imaginative use of large cabochon-cut gemstones, rock crystal and enamel heightened with star sapphires and rubies. As an English jeweller, Frederick Partridge belongs to the Arts and Crafts tradition; certainly William Morris and his associates must have admired his skilful working of horn. Yet Partridge was much impressed by the French jewellers, especially by the way they cleverly worked this humble material up into a thing

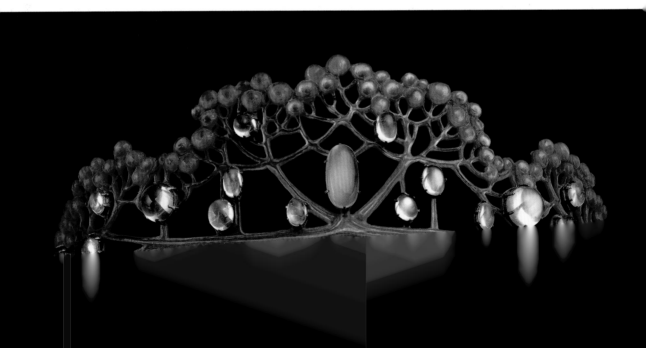

of beauty. Sadly, his output was not prolific, but the few tiaras of his that have survived are touchingly poetic and exquisitely beautiful (Plate 58).

In direct contrast to the followers of the Arts and Crafts tradition, jewellers who espoused Art Nouveau rejected historicism completely. Such a clean break with the past meant that art was free to return to nature for inspiration, and the exponents of the movement believed that this was where real truth and beauty were to be found. Although John Ruskin had promoted such a move for many years, an exotic catalyst was required before artists felt able to accept this new vision, and it came in the unexpected form of Japanese art. Japan had been a virtually closed country since the 17th century because its rulers feared the corrupting effects of foreign influences. Only after persistent pressure from the West, at the end of the Edo period (1615–1868), did the Emperor open Japanese ports to foreign trade. When the first works of art found their way to Europe and America, craftsmen were awed by the way in which Japanese artists had managed to portray nature: exactly, minutely, and sometimes in a state of imperfection. In addition to this, a wealth of new materials and techniques now presented themselves, but one in particular lent itself to this fresh vision of nature: a type of cloisonné enamel from which the back plate had been removed. It was called 'plique à jour' and, being transparent, it proved ideal for the representation of all sorts organic material, including the veining of leaves, the petals of flowers and the gauzy wings of insects.

René Lalique (1860–1945) was undoubtedly the greatest master of these techniques, as he was the genius of the Art

58 A tiara carved from cow's horn in the form of elderberries, to which cling moonstone dewdrops. By Frederick Partridge, c. 1900. Partridge's work, always hauntingly poetic, is more French in character than it is English. His jewellery was retailed by Liberty. Private Collection.

Nouveau movement as a whole. Nature seen through Lalique's eyes is often a disquieting vision. Gone are the balance and symmetry of the classical wreaths and garlands of antiquity; in their place are sinuous arrangements of shrubs and plants wrenched from the ground, or torn straight from the branch. The sensual beauty of a flower-head, rendered in ivory or horn, may be disturbed by the presence of a foraging insect. Sometimes the conventional form of the tiara is lost in these feverishly inspired works of art, and its weight has to be supported like a helmet round the head. When Lalique died, Calouste Gulbenkian, his most important patron, wrote a letter of condolence to his daughter, in which he said: 'He ranks amongst the greatest figures in the history of Art of all time, and his personal masterly touch, his exquisite imagination, will excite the admiration of future elites.'

Had it not been for the overshadowing genius of Lalique, Georges Fouquet (1862–1957) would be remembered as the most talented Art Nouveau jeweller. His collaboration with the painter Alphonse Mucha resulted in the creation of some remarkable pieces, and these were shown at the Exposition Universelle of 1900. Fouquet, too, was fascinated by the plant world, and made numerous orchids, cornflowers and sycamore seeds of plique-à-jour enamel.

Because the emphasis fell on design rather than intrinsic worth, new techniques and materials, including aluminium (first produced industrially in 1854), were particularly fascinating to the Art Nouveau artists and craftsmen. Lalique, for one, was especially interested in them, and was quick to recognize the potential of lighter materials in the making of head ornaments.

A number of highly gifted jewellers were working in Paris at the turn of the century, the majority of them in the Art Nouveau style. Although not many of

59 A tiara comb bodice ornament in the form of sweet peas, made by René Lalique, Paris, c.1903. The heads of these fragrant flowers are cleverly evoked with cast glass and their nectar with faceted topaz. The body of the comb is made of carved bleached horn, and the flower stems and leaves are created with enamel and plique-à-jour enamel. The Victoria and Albert Museum Picture Library.

60, 61 Designs by Boucheron, c.1890. The tiara shown in the top drawing is to be set with an opal and five rows of pearls suspended between diamond and pearl set supports, whilst the one below will bear eleven conch pearls supported on a gallery of brilliant diamonds. Boucheron, Paris.

them were making head ornaments (possibly because France was a republic once again), the firms of Maison Vever, René Foy and Lucien Gaillard are of particular note. Both Henri Vever and René Foy exhibited dramatic tiaras at the Exposition Universelle in 1900. Vever's pieces were a tangle of seed pods, and another took the form of fern fronds that cling to the shape of the head. Foy's was an enamelled peacock feather, which spreads out over the hair. Galliard, whose jewellery mirrors Lalique's quite closely in its treatment of nature, employed Japanese craftsmen to carve horn and make patinated metals and enamel work to heighten the effect of his combs, wreaths and diadems.

Frédéric Boucheron had a higher regard for the intrinsic value of a piece than other designers of the time, and it is for this reason that so few of his firm's remarkable jewels have survived intact. Boucheron tiaras, set with fine diamonds and coloured stones, were invariably broken up when the tide of fashion changed so that the precious stones could be reused elsewhere. In some instances, when a piece failed to find a buyer with a personality equal to the eccentricity of a design, it was the craftsmen themselves who were given the soul-destroying task of dismantling their own breathtakingly beautiful creations. The photographic records preserved at the firm's premises in Paris (Plates 62–66) provide an eloquent testimony to Boucheron's very particular contribution to the history of French jewellery.

One of the defining characteristics of Art Nouveau jewellery was that its function was secondary to its appeal as a work of art. In this respect jewellery at the end of the 19th century had regained the status it had enjoyed in the Renaissance, hundreds of years before. But there could be little future for a type of jewellery that could not be easily worn.

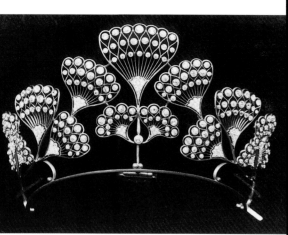

63 *(left)* A unique pierced gold and diamond diadem, painted black to simulate lace, made by Menu in June 1891 for Boucheron. It failed to sell and was taken apart in May 1902. Boucheron, Paris.

64 *(below)* A diadem made by Boucheron in the form of twinned lily flowers and a bud, the petals and stamens entirely set with brilliant- and rose-cut diamonds. c.1900. Boucheron, Paris.

62 *(above)* A pierced gold tiara in the form of stylized foliage set with brilliant diamonds, made by Boucheron in July 1904. Boucheron, Paris.

66 *(left)* A platinum tiara in the form of twinned feathers tied to a diamond-set bandeau with a brilliant-cut stone of 2.5 carats. One feather is of black onyx with a diamond-set quill, the other of diamonds with an onyx quill. Most of the stones used in this highly imaginative composition have been cut especially for it. Made for stock in November 1920, it remained unsold until February 1925, when it was taken apart. Boucheron, Paris.

65 *(right)* A diamond-set tiara in the form of a kokoshnik, the stylized motifs based on a Scythian ornament. Made by Le Saché for Boucheron in 1906. It was unsold and taken apart in February 1909. Boucheron, Paris.

67 A pierced gold tiara in the form of a frieze of graduated cyclamen leaves and flowers tied with ribbons, c.1900. The tiara can be removed from its frame and worn upside-down as a necklace. A rare example of a gem-set tiara in the Art Nouveau taste by Fabergé, originally owned by Mrs Wilson Fox. Their Graces the Duke and Duchess of Westminster.

68 *(right)* A tiara decorated with black enamel and paste that supports a spray of egret's feathers. French, c.1910. Madeleine Popper.

69 *(below)* A design by E. Wolff & Co. showing a tiara in the form of exploding fireworks, to be set with diamonds and coloured stones, 1907. E. Wolfe & Co., London.

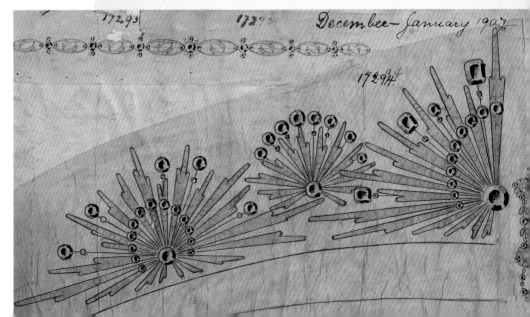

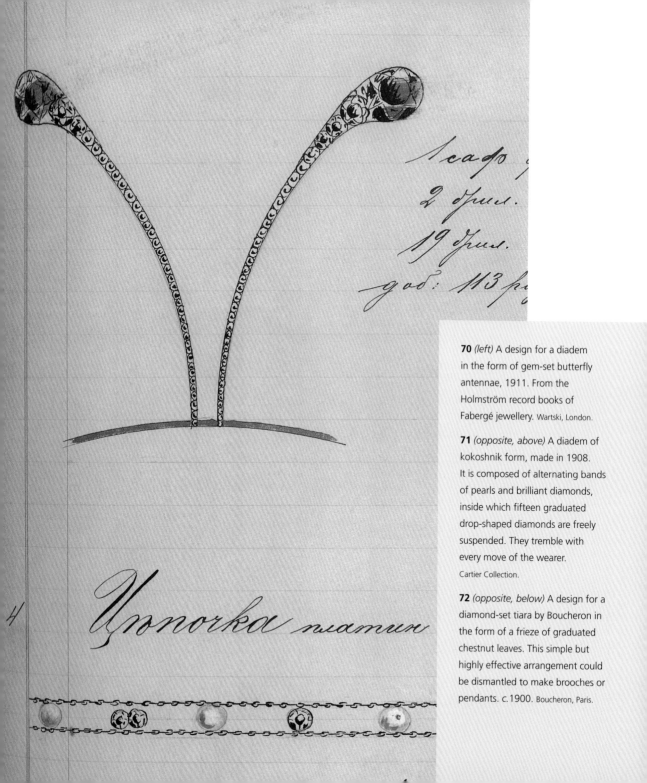

Цепочка платин

4

70 *(left)* A design for a diadem in the form of gem-set butterfly antennae, 1911. From the Holmström record books of Fabergé jewellery. Wartski, London.

71 *(opposite, above)* A diadem of kokoshnik form, made in 1908. It is composed of alternating bands of pearls and brilliant diamonds, inside which fifteen graduated drop-shaped diamonds are freely suspended. They tremble with every move of the wearer. Cartier Collection.

72 *(opposite, below)* A design for a diamond-set tiara by Boucheron in the form of a frieze of graduated chestnut leaves. This simple but highly effective arrangement could be dismantled to make brooches or pendants. c.1900. Boucheron, Paris.

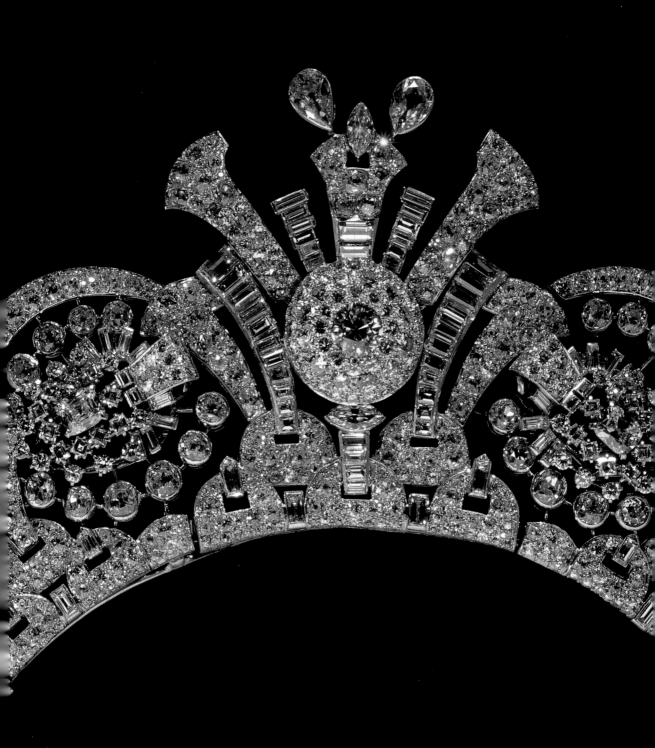

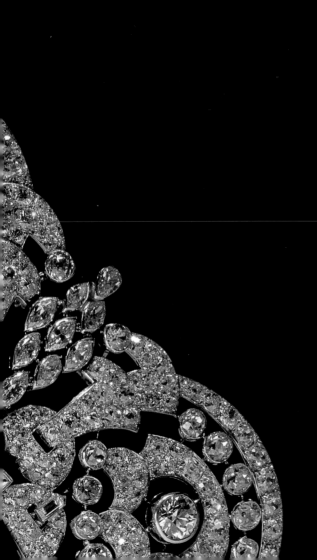

ART DECO

ALTHOUGH its origins may be traced back to the turn of the century, the Art Deco movement takes its name from the Exposition des Arts Décoratifs et Modernes, the first exhibition of decorative arts to be held after the First World War. It was staged in Paris in 1925 and the artists who contributed to it aimed to supplant the Art Nouveau style with a modern geometric scheme that echoed the advances of the Machine Age. René Lalique demonstrated his virtuosity as a designer by exhibiting his work alongside that of the couturier Paul Poiret and the silversmith Jean Puifocat. It is ironic, however, that some of the most exciting pieces of this period were not based on modernism after all, but on the more exotic sources that had inspired much of the work of the late 19th century.

The fortunes of the jewellery trade at this time were greatly affected by the economic difficulties that followed Black Thursday, 12 October 1929. Financial institutions collapsed throughout the world, bankruptcies spiralled and unrest quickly followed. Jewellers had to cope not only with the fall in custom but also with the blight of unpaid debt.

The dress designer Coco Chanel did her best to dispel the gloom by creating a highly imaginative range of jewellery, which she showed at her hotel in the Fauberg-Saint-Honoré in 1932. Here she assembled a collection of mannequins adorned with diadems in the form of comets and stars, their foreheads hung with articulated diamond-set fringes. Through her amorous association with the 2nd Duke of Westminster, Chanel knew perfectly well that there were certain individuals whose wealth was so enormous that it could sustain almost

73 Mrs Wilfrid Ashley, stepmother of Edwina Mountbatten, who was to become Lady Mount Temple when her husband succeeded to the title in 1932. Here she is wearing an extraordinary array of emerald beads as a necklace, an armband, a brooch worn at the hip and a tiara by Cartier (Plate 76). The photograph was taken at the Jewels of Empire Ball in 1930. Cartier, London.

74, 75 The tiara designed by Lacloche as a gift from the 2nd Duke of Westminster to his wife, Loelia Ponsonby, when they married in 1930. It was once set with three immense stones called the Hastings and Arcot diamonds. A detachable diamond rivière necklace ran along its outer border. A strong Chinese influence can be detected not only in the form of this jewel but also in the way it is positioned on the head, parallel to the face. This tiara, and the photograph taken by Cecil Beaton of the Duchess wearing it *(opposite)*, are amongst the greatest masterpieces of the Art Deco movement. I Fischzang, New York. Cecil Beaton photograph courtesy of Sotheby's London.

any financial shock. Nonetheless the international mood of frugality seems to have affected even the Duke when, in 1930, he asked the famous French firm of Lacloche to make up a tiara in the Chinese taste for his fourth wife, Loelia. In the interests of economy, several family jewels were broken up to furnish the required number of stones, and at its centre blazed three of largest diamonds in his collection (Plates 74, 75).

Despite feeling the brutal pinch inflicted by the crash of 1929, noble families were expected to maintain their traditional place in society. An outmoded tiara must have seemed just as unappealing as an unfashionable dress, so those who had social obligations but no longer the means to maintain them ordered head ornaments set with less valuable yet nonetheless decorative gemstones. Aquamarines took the place of sapphires and the humble citrine mimicked the effect of precious topaz. Whatever the materials selected by the customer, the skilled craftsmen working at this difficult time were still able to transform them into masterpieces of the jeweller's art.

The Westminster tiara was designed in an unconventional way, so that it could be worn across the head from ear to ear. This was just one of several methods devised by Art Deco jewellers to secure tiaras to the shorter hairstyles of the 20th century. In some instances, new shapes broke all conventions by circling the forehead, dropping below the ears and framing the back of the head. A good proportion of these Art Deco head ornaments displayed a versatility that was characteristic of many 19th-century tiaras; with the twist of a small screwdriver the jewel-work could be detached from the frame and converted easily into a flexible necklace, bracelets or the double clips that were so fashionable at the time.

76 A striking Art Deco tiara made by Cartier in 1928 in the Indian taste, in homage to the probable origins of the carved emerald and twenty-one emerald beads with which it is set. The central element of this remarkable jewel takes the form of a horned mask that can be detached from the diamond bandeau and worn separately. The Art Deco movement assimilated many influences from the Far East, especially from China and Japan. This is one of the most exciting examples of the style ever made. Cartier, London.

77 A platinum sunburst tiara made by Cartier in 1927 for Countess Tysckiewicz. Its striking design is accentuated by the use of alternating bands of brilliant- and rose-cut diamonds. The central element is *tremblant* and was once set with a jonquil-coloured diamond which was later replaced by a large star sapphire. Several versions of this jewel were made, by different Parisian jewellers; when Princess Irina Youssoupova was on honeymoon in Paris in 1914, she ordered one from Chaumet. Private Collection.

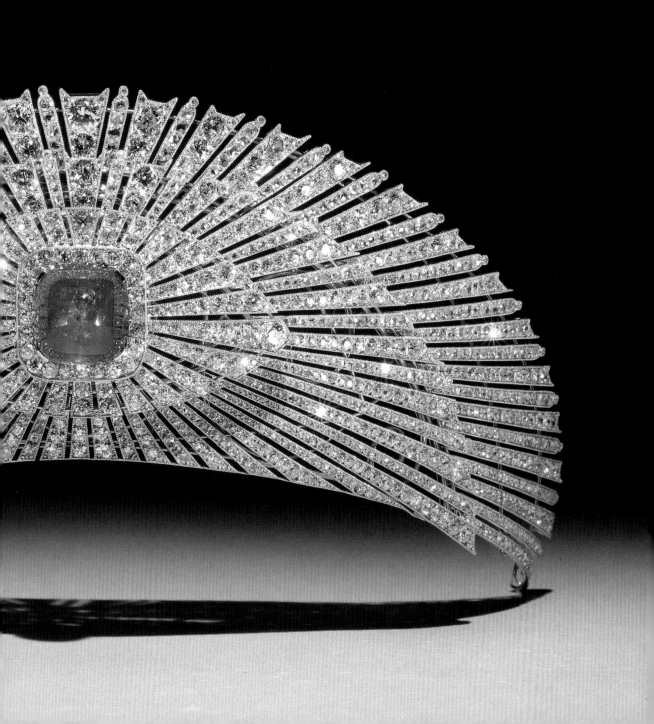

The coronation of George VI in 1937 ensured that many tiaras were made and worn that year. Cartier, who created so many of the most memorable Art Deco tiaras, was alone responsible for twenty-seven, which probably made their appearance at the social events held to celebrate the new reign. In the long term, however, the pre-war period marked the start of the tiara's decline. When the roof leaked it was not the family silver but the family tiara that was first to go. Vast numbers were sold for little more than their intrinsic value, and most were broken up to make innumerable single-stone engagement rings.

Few could possibly have imagined then that by the end of what would prove such a troubled century, there would be a revival of interest in the tiara. Still less might they have guessed the direction which this, the most exciting expression of the jeweller's art, would take.

78 A tortoiseshell bandeau made by Cartier in 1928. It is set with diamond and pearl-set flower heads and bordered with calibre-cut gemstones. Cartier, London.

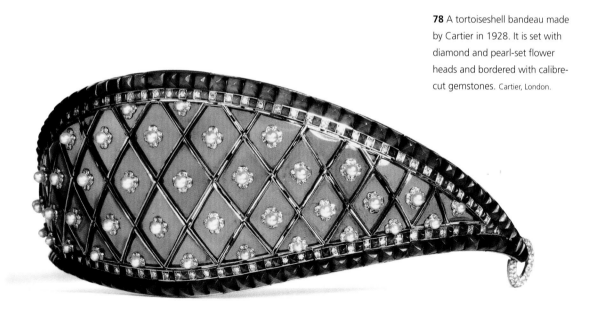

79 A truly magnificent tiara of oriental inspiration, made by Cartier for Countess Granard in 1937. Its sweeping line is accentuated by parallel rows of calibré sapphires. Brilliant and pear-shaped stones of great value are incorporated into the design; some are old-cut, and must have come from the Granard family collection. Lady Granard was an American heiress with a legendary appetite for jewellery and the funds to satisfy it. Cartier, London.

80 *(opposite)* A diamond-set tiara of oriental inspiration, designed to be worn around the face rather than on top of the head. It was ordered from Cartier in 1937.
Cartier, London.

81, 82 *(above and right)* A diamond-set bandeau decorated with carved turquoise in the Persian taste. This clever adaptation of a jewel originally made by Boucheron was bought by Viscount Astor from Cartier in 1930.
Cartier, London.

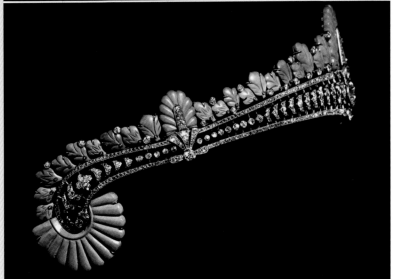

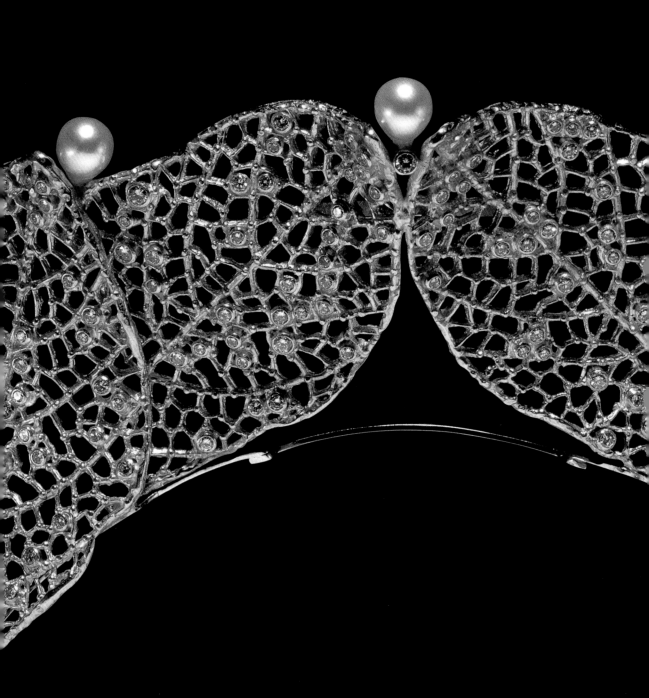

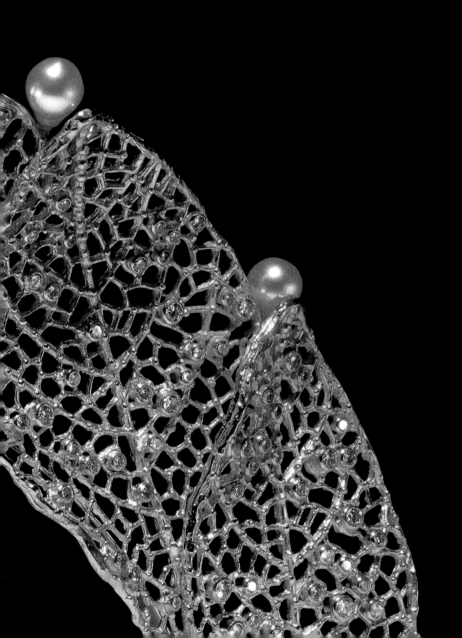

the TIARA TODAY

NOW that celebrity has been accorded almost royal status in society today, it is rather fitting that stars of the media are showing so much enthusiasm for the tiara, and look set to endorse it as an item of high fashion entering a new and exciting phase of design.

The first television personality to recognize the exciting potential of the tiara was the late Paula Yates. She saw it as a curiosity, a fashion accessory, but above all, in the post-punk era of the 1980s, as an object of irony. Her tiaras were not set with diamonds, and were not worn with the finest silk evening dresses. Hers were set with worthless rhinestones and she sported them with her faded jeans or her (very) mini skirts. It is difficult to know what brought the tiara to the attention of the fashion-conscious once again, but the subversion of all things royal by the punk aesthetic at the time of the Silver Jubilee may have helped. Vivienne Westwood, once queen of punk couture, and now haute couturier, owns a 19th-century Italian coral diadem decorated with Turkey oak leaves and acorns and has enjoyed wearing it not only at the finale of her catwalk shows but also when bicycling around London. Vivienne has adorned the heads of her models with a variety of tiaras. Some are made of brightly coloured plastic and break every convention, as they swirl around the head and fall completely out of symmetry. Others are patinated with copper and in their extreme severity evoke the diadems of ancient Sparta (Plate 88). For the exhibition of tiaras held at Wartski in aid of The Samaritans in 1997 she made a diadem in the form of a gift-wrapped dog's bone (Plate 87).

The late Gianni Versace, favourite clothes designer of the rock stars, won the de Beers International Award in 1996 with a tiara set with diamonds valued at £1.5 million. It was lent to Madonna on several occasions, but for her wedding

83 Madonna wearing Versace's diamond tiara. It is centred on a mask of Medusa (one of Versace's favourite emblems), supported by a Greek meander surmounted by vine leaves. Versace. Photograph by Mario Testino.

to Guy Ritchie in December 2000 she chose a conventional late 19th-century diamond tiara borrowed from Asprey & Garrard, set with diamonds weighing 78 carats and arranged as floral garlands. It beautifully complemented her wedding dress, designed for her by Stella McCartney. With the same sense of style-consciousness, Elton John has taken an interest in the tiara. The two rhinestone diadems he bought in a cheap bridal shop in Los Angeles were the inspiration for the title of the biographical film, *Tantrums and Tiaras*, made by his friend David Furnish in 1996. Elton John lent them to Wartski's exhibition in 1997, where they were the focus of considerable press attention (Plate 84).

In Hollywood, tiaras have recently been adorning the heads of famous actresses, including Sharon Stone, Meg Ryan and Minnie Driver. Elizabeth Hurley, meanwhile, inverted the girlish charm of the floral wreath by wearing one woven not from daisy chains but of barbed wire. Another Hollywood star, Jamie Lee Curtis, has recently acquired a new tiara, but the circumstances on

84 A rhinestone and base metal tiara in the form of a star flanked with foliage. This was the jewel that inspired the title of the biographical film *Tantrums and Tiaras* (1996) made by David Furnish about his friend Elton John. Sir Elton John and David Furnish.

this occasion were more traditional. As the wife of the hereditary baron, Lord Haden-Guest, she attended the State Opening of Parliament in 1998. She asked her friend Cathy Waterman to design the mandatory tiara, which took the form of a simple but highly effective wreath of gold leaves.

Slim Barratt, winner of the 2000 de Beers International Award, has designed a number of head ornaments, some set with diamonds. Perhaps his most famous commission was the circlet he made for Victoria Adams ('Posh Spice') when she married David Beckham in 1999, which was subsequently lent to the Victoria and Albert Museum. This was not the first time the Museum demonstrated its interest in contemporary tiara design. Seeming to anticipate the tiara's renaissance, it acquired a diadem of silver wire decorated with beads of ivory, rock crystal and mother of pearl as far back as 1980. It had been made by the American-born jeweller Frances Bendixon earlier that year. The Museum has also maintained a close association with the goldsmith and jeweller Wendy Ramshaw, who has made a series of highly imaginative head-dresses of silver and gold heightened with enamel and the feathers of all manner of exotic birds, including the emu.

Not all the tiaras made today are as overtly contemporary. Ilias Lalaounis, the jeweller based in Athens, makes wreaths and diadems set with precious stones inspired by the head ornaments of antiquity. In 1969, when the fashion for tiaras was probably at its lowest ebb, his firm made a tiara in the Minoan taste, followed in 1975 by a diadem in Byzantine style intended for the Shah of Iran. In 1983 it made a head ornament called 'Helen', made up of articulated gold panels and based on the gold jewellery of Helen of Troy found by Heinrich Schliemann in 1873.

All these remarkable art jewels are very different from their gem-set cousins made by the old established firms of London, Paris and New York. Owing to the high cost of precious jewellery, Garrard, Cartier and Tiffany were quick to notice the lack of demand for tiaras after the Second World War and to respond in the necessary manner. Nonetheless, they were asked to make some head ornaments in the traditional fashion from time to time. Orders tended to come not from Europe, but from the courts of more exotic monarchies.

85 *(above)* A tiara made in 2001 by Elizabeth Gage in the form of skeleton leaves set with diamonds and topped with five pearls. Elizabeth Gage.

86 *(below)* An English gold tiara in the form of graduated clusters of leaves and flowers set with diamonds in platinum, c.1890. It was worn by Miss Betty Boothroyd, Speaker of the House of Commons 1992–2000. Photograph Wartski.

Today the retail jewellers of the West End of London are making gem-set tiaras once more. Again the demand for them is believed to come, at least in part, from the Near and Far East, where they remain a popular part of bridal wear. Few of these bright new jewels have the versatility of their predecessors, which could be converted with relative ease into brooches and necklaces, but their luminously beautiful precious stones, in particular coloured diamonds, ensure that they still create a dramatic effect. The best can be found at Asprey & Garrard, Cartier, Boucheron, David Morris and Graff.

Although it is reassuring to know that traditional gem-set tiaras are still being made by the most prestigious firms, and exciting to see the inspired creations of contemporary designers, the future of the tiara lies in the public appreciation of these uniquely attractive jewels. At the moment, things are looking promising; tiaras are generating enthusiasm and curiosity whenever they are seen; books and exhibitions proliferate; and we can only hope that the Queen's Golden Jubilee sparks off new and exciting developments in the long and fascinating design history of the tiara.

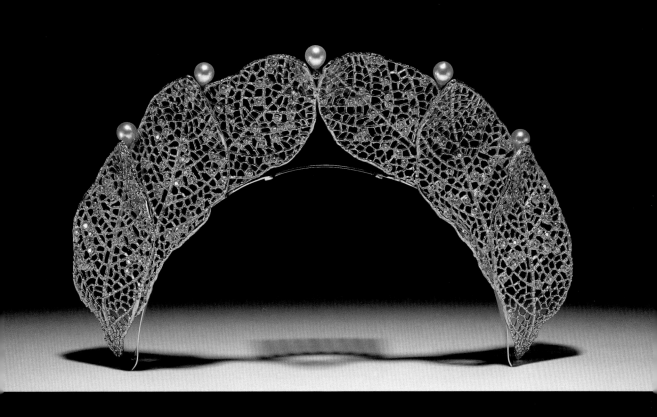

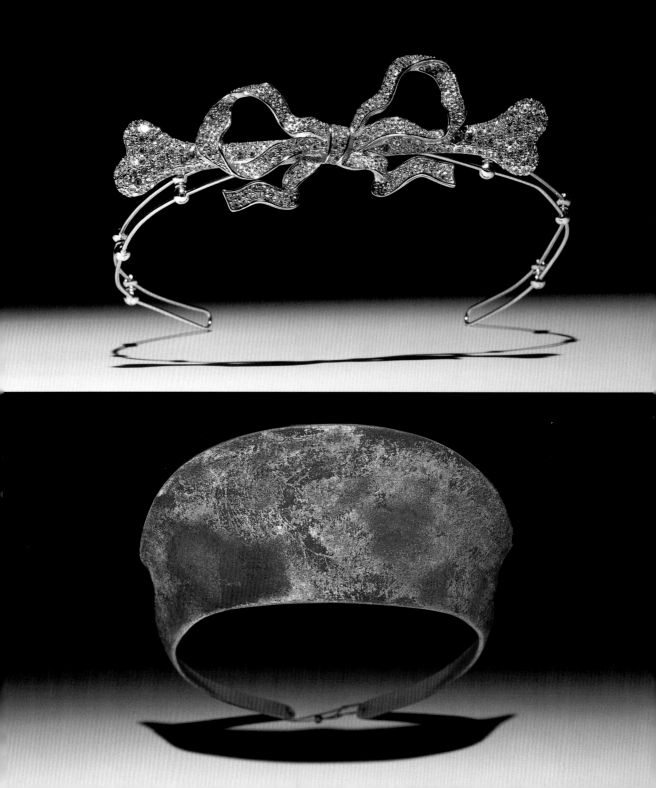

87, 88, 89 Three tiaras designed by Vivienne Westwood. *(Opposite, above)* A rhinestone tiara in the form of a dog's bone tied with a bow; *(opposite, below)* a neo-classical Spartan tiara in acrylic patinated with gold; and *(right)* a yellow acrylic tiara in the form of clouds of ribbon. Vivienne Westwood. Photograph *(right)* by Ugo Camera.

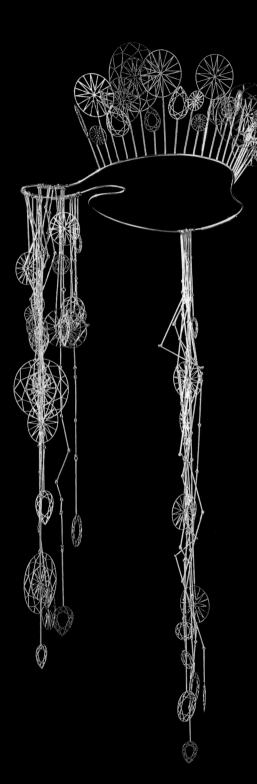

90 A dramatic tiara of pierced openwork by the goldsmith and jeweller Wendy Ramshaw. Starbursts and diamond-shaped pendants hang from the temples in a way that evokes the ancient splendour of Byzantium. 2001. Wendy Ramshaw.

91, 92 An openwork gold tiara by Jan Mandel, designed as part of a series of 'transformation' jewels that can be taken apart and worn as a necklace, brooches and earrings. Made in 2001, this dramatic jewel is redolent of the flares of the sun seen during an eclipse. Jan Mandel.

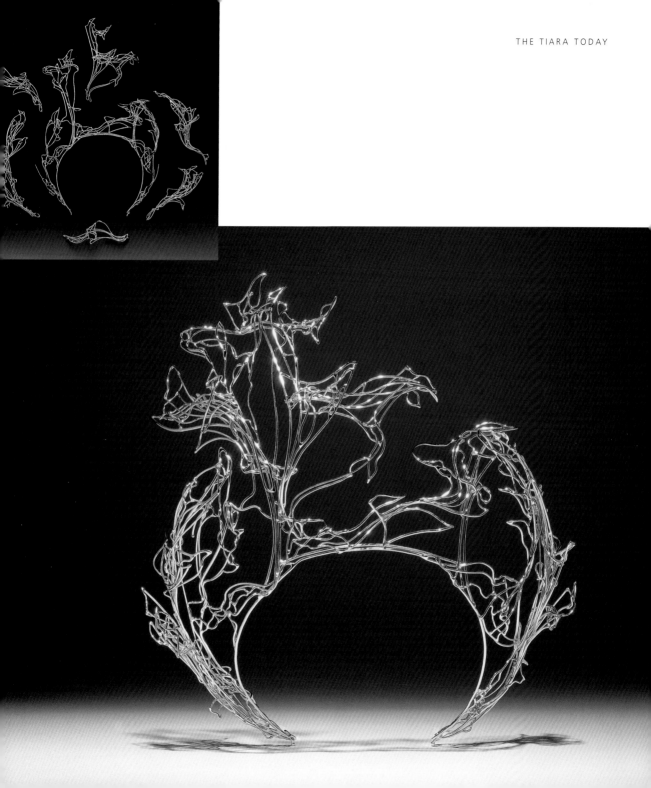

93, 94 A beechwood tiara designed by Tim Gosling for David Linley Furniture. The tiara takes the form of autumn leaves carved from beechwood and washed, and was designed for 'Tiaras', the exhibition at the Victoria and Albert Museum held in 2002, the year of the Golden Jubilee. The photograph of Viscountess Linley wearing the tiara was taken by her father-in-law, Lord Snowdon. Snowdon, and David Linley Furniture.

95 (opposite) An 18-carat gold tiara set with green quartz, citrines and green pearls, designed by Prince Dimitri of Yugoslavia in 2001. The tiara was designed to support detachable aigrettes. His Highness Prince Dimitri of Yugoslavia.

96 *(opposite)* 'American Tiara: Invasive Species', made from oxidized sterling silver and 18 carat gold, in 2001. A tangle of urban weeds, none of which is native to America, this tiara is described by its designer, Jan Yager, as 'A testament to the beauty and power of nature, and tangible evidence of a hundred years of trade between nations.' Courtesy of the artist.

97 *(right)* Jasmine Guinness wearing a tiara from Philip Treacy's 1999 Haute Couture collection, shown in London and New York, made from hand-curled, specially treated feathers and Swarovski crystals. Photograph © Robert Fairer.

Further Reading

Arwas, Victor, *Art Deco* (1980, London)

Becker, Vivienne, *Art Nouveau Jewellery* (1985, London)

Bury, Shirley, *Jewellery 1789–1910* (1991, Woodbridge)

Corson, Richard, *Fashions in Hair – The First Five Thousand Years* (1965, London)

Field, Leslie, *The Jewels of Queen Elizabeth II – Her Personal Collection* (1992, London)

Fregnac Claude, *Jewellery from the Renaissance to Art Nouveau* (1965, London)

Gere, Charlotte, *Victorian Jewellery Design* (1972, London)
—, *European and American Jewellery 1830–1914* (1975, London)
—, and John Culme, *Garrard the Crown Jewellers for 150 Years* (1993, London)
—, and Geoffrey C. Munn, *Artists Jewellery* (1989, Woodbridge)

Habsburg, Geza von, and Marina Lopato, *Fabergé – Imperial Jeweller* (1994, London)

Higgins, Reynold, *Greek and Roman Jewellery* (1961, London)

Hinks, Peter, *Twentieth-Century Jewellery 1900–1980* (1983, London)
—, *Nineteenth-Century Jewellery* (1985, London)

Hughes, Graham, *Marit Aschan – Enamellist of our Time* (1995, London)

International Exhibition of Modern Jewellery, Exhibition Catalogue (1961, Worshipful Company of Goldsmiths)

Jenkyns, Richard, *The Victorians and Ancient Greece* (1980, Oxford)

Kiste, John van der, *Crowns in a Changing World – The British and European Monarchies 1901–36* (1993, London)

Kunz, George Frederick and Charles Hugh Stevenson, *The Book of the Pearl* (1908, New York)

Lightbown, Ronald, *Mediaeval European Jewellery* (1992, London)

Marshall F. H., *Catalogue of the Jewellery, Greek, Etruscan, and Roman in the Department of Antiquities,* British Museum (1911, London)

Menkes, Suzy, *The Royal Jewels* (1985, London)

Moynahan, Brian, *The British Century – A Photographic History of the Last Two Hundred Years* (1999, London)

Munn, Geoffrey C., *Castellani and Giuliano – Revivalist Jewellers of the Nineteenth Century* (1984, London)

Nadelhoffer, Hans, *Cartier – Jewellers Extraordinary* (1984, London)

Néret, Gilles, *Boucheron – Four Generations of a World-Renowned Jeweler* (1988, New York)

Pepper, Terence, *High Society Photographs 1897–1914* (1998, London)

Proddow, Penny and Marion Fasel, *Diamonds – A Century of Spectacular Jewels* (1996, New York)

Proddow, P., P. Healy and M. Fasel, *Hollywood Jewels, Movies, Jewelry, Stars* (1992, New York)

Phillips, Clare, *Jewellery from Antiquity until the Present Day* (1996, London),
—, *Jewels and Jewellery* (2000, London)

Scarisbrick, Diana, *Ancestral Jewellery* (1989, London),
—, *Jewellery in Britain 1066–1837* (1994, London.)
—, *Chaumet, Master Jewellers Since 1780* (1995, Paris)
—, *Tiara* (2000, San Francisco)

Snowman, A. Kenneth (ed.), *The Master Jewellers* (1990, London)
—, *Fabergé: Lost and Found. The Recently Discovered Jewelry Design Books of the St. Petersburg Archives* (1993, New York)

Twining, Lord E.F., *A History of the Crown Jewels of Europe* (1960, London)

Young, Sheila, *The Queen's Jewellery* (1968, London)

98 A platinum tiara set with diamonds in the Louis XVI taste, shown here as a flexible necklace. This extremely versatile jewel, made by Cartier, 1907, consists of five different elements, and may also be worn as a circular diamond pendant, hair combs and bracelets.
Private Collection.